Planted to Produce
7 Shifts to Activate Your Creative Soul

By Ticora Davis, Esq.

Copyright © 2019 by Ticora Davis

ISBN: 970-0-578-62190-6

Editor: Jasmine Womack

For more information, please visit: www.ticoradavis.com

Because of the dynamic nature of the internet, any web addresses or links contained in this book may have changed since publication and may no longer be valid.

Dedication Page

To my husband, Tyrone,

to my children, Miles & Gianna,

to Daddy & Mommy,

and

to Revolutionary Creative

I am anchored by your roots.

Bonus Content

Planted to Produce Worksheets

- Access bonus chapter worksheets

Behind the Book Videos

- View inspirational chapter videos

Planted to Produce: The Experience

- Receive exclusive training to help you shift, activate your creative soul, and bring this book to life

All bonus resources, videos and training can be found at www.ticoradavis.com/resources

Table of Contents

Introduction

I once felt like a pebble carelessly tossed into the center of a lake skipping the surface of the waters and left to sink to the bottom of the merciless pit.

Cold. Alone. Forgotten.

One of the most deceptive lies you can believe is that you are the only person in the world struggling to shift out of your sunken place. It is soul crushing to believe that you are the only pebble at the bottom of the lake. This single belief kept me bound in a state of depression for five years. This belief sabotaged relationships, my self worth, and my faith in Christ. This belief convinced me I was unworthy of love, joy, change, and triumph and bound me by the shackles of fear, shame, and stagnation.

That is until one day I made the revolutionary choice to change my life. Through the grace of God and my grit, I went from being an almost-college drop out to the owner of a successful trademark law firm, business consultant, sought after speaker, and, now, author.

As I went through the process of saving myself, I met many amazing men and women of God who used spiritual keys to unlock my healing, forgiveness, and ultimate transformation.

This book is your key.

Every chapter was written to unlock a new level in you, shift you out of being stuck, and activate your creative soul.

Like you, I was never forgotten. I was not buried. I was hidden under the safety of my Heavenly Father's wings.

I was planted with the sole purpose to produce everything in me. It is my prayer that as you read and experience this book you will shift spiritually, physically, emotionally, financially and mentally into being a co-creator with God.

You've stayed at this mountain long enough. (Deuteronomy 1:6)

It's time to shift.

Chapter 1

Dormant

*"Very truly I tell you, unless a kernel of wheat falls
to the ground and dies, it remains only a single seed.
But if it dies, it produces many seeds."*
- John 12:24 (NIV)

If you've ever taken a trip to the gardening store, you've likely seen a pack of seeds. Despite the type of seed, they are always dry inside the pack. Dry seeds are what you'd call *dormant*. As a former botanist, dormant is a *term of art* in the field which means "temporarily inactive."

No matter how long those seeds are in the pack, it doesn't change what the seeds are and what they can potentially become. A pumpkin seed in the pack and a pumpkin seed in the ground are the same. The only thing that changed was its environment. A change in your environment is sometimes the only thing you need to move you from a season of dormancy to a lifetime of flourishing.

The image on the front of the packet of seeds is your intended form and who God ultimately wants you to be.

God will show you yourself just so you can remember who you are.

God will show you yourself just so you can hold on.

God will show you a glimpse of yourself in the future just so you can survive your present season.

You may have picked up this book because you feel like you're lost, in a pit, or encountering a valley. You may be experiencing depression, darkness, struggles, and quite frankly, feeling as if you have been buried. According to Merriam-Webster, the definition of 'bury' is 'to dispose of by depositing in the earth; to conceal [or] cover with earth; or to conceal in obscurity.'

When you bury anything, the intent is to ensure it is deliberately forgotten.

Do you feel as if you have been forgotten? Do you feel that your gifts have been concealed by the challenges of your life? Do you feel as if you have been buried?

I know that feeling all too well. I was convinced that I had been buried when in reality, I had been planted.

Perhaps you too have been planted.

To plant means to "put or set in the ground for growth; to set or sow with seeds; to establish; or to conceal."

When people meet you they do not know where you are on your life's journey. Even more often, people have a tendency to mischaracterize the purpose behind your concealment.

They simply believe that because you are in your underdog phase, because you are in the ground, that you have been buried, not planted.

They have no idea whether your seeds have just been planted in the ground, whether you are erupting through the earth to blossom, or whether you are in full bloom.

For those of us experiencing darkness, we are in our seed phase.

Some seeds grow fast. All they need is a little water, a little love, rich soil and they burst through the soil and grow rapidly. Other seeds, like Chinese Bamboo, may take a very long time to burst through the earth. Oh but when they do, they grow faster and stronger than any other plant.

So just because you're in a dark place, just because you're struggling, just because you don't know exactly what your next steps are, it doesn't mean that you have been buried. I am suggesting that have been planted.

In 2008, God revealed this to me. At that time, I was in the midst of a depression. I remember sitting on my couch, and I was struggling. I would go to lay down, and I would cry out to God while holding onto my Bible and I would plead, "Lord, help me."

I was desperate for change.

My soul continued to cry, "I can't function and I'm having a hard time getting up in the morning. I'm having a hard time. I'm having a hard time. God, I'm having a hard time. I procrastinate all the time. I can't do what I've been called to do."

I continued to question everything while asking myself, *Why am I struggling? God, what is wrong with me?*

It was then that God showed me a vision of myself in the future. In a glimpse, He showed me me. The "me" He always saw. The "me" I could not see. In the vision, I saw myself on a stage speaking to tons of people.

He said, "You are going to help people overcome what you're going through. You're going to help people overcome procrastination, shame, indecision and fear."

And in my pain, I got so upset and so offended with God. I became angry towards God because I thought that was mean and extremely cruel. I expected that God would show me me, but in a different way.

In my anger, I questioned, "God, how can I help people when I can't help myself? How can I help people overcome procrastination when I struggle with procrastination, shame, indecision and fear?"

Do you know that God will show you yourself so that you can survive? He's not showing you yourself so you can suffer. He's not showing you your dreams and visions to be cruel. He is showing you yourself so you can survive the season that you're in.

That is why God is showing you, and that is why God is giving you dreams and visions. That is why God is telling you there is so much bigger than your present season. That is why God is giving you these visions, dreams and these things that blow your mind; it's why you see visions of yourself doing things that you've never seen before that you cannot even believe that you wonder, *how can I do that*?

He is showing you yourself so you can survive. He is not being cruel.

I now realize when I speak to people on and offline about procrastination, how people take what I say and they obtain a bit more freedom and they give themselves a little more grace. They share that my words blow their mind, that I am helping them, and that they needed to hear my message.

A young lady told me, "Ticora, you posted a status a year ago and it changed my life. As a result, I went to my therapist, and now I have the tools along with a new mindset, and I am healthier."

As I read these comments now and have these experiences, I often think, "Oh my God, it's happening."

I am what I saw.

I am who I saw.

I am right now living the life of the woman I saw 10 years ago in the midst of my depression.

You don't know when you're going to wake up and realize you're in the middle of living the life that at one time, you dreamt of. Even if you are in a dark place, struggling, and cannot see your way out, know that God is still birthing the dreams inside of you...not being cruel to you. He is showing you YOU so you can survive. You have what it takes to get through your valley and get to the place where He wants you to go.

God loves you very, very much, but he knows that you need this season that you're in right now, and He needs you to press your way through it.

I see that in this season, the vision God showed me is slowly coming to fruition. I see the miracle manifesting now. I don't know how everything is going to happen, but the how isn't really important. Pastor Rona Williams shared with our congregation one day, "It is not your job to manage the miracle."

I share that gem with you right now. Do not try to micromanage the God-sized miracles for your life. It is not your job to worry about how everything is going to happen. Do not worry about how things are going to work out. Do not worry about the little steps that you need to take to get there. Be obedient day to day, minute to minute, hour to hour, press forward, and take strides to inch closer to your dreams. I don't care if you have to crawl or run, you will be required to move and do the hard work to get from the YOU that you are today to the YOU you want to be in the future. As you move, the miracle will begin to happen.

Spiritual Reasons Behind Procrastination

While most discussions surrounding the root cause of procrastination tend to focus on psychological or behavioral factors, we cannot ignore the spiritual shifts that cause you to procrastinate.

If you are struggling with procrastination, somewhere throughout your life demonic influences found a way to plant seeds of doubt, fear, and shame in your soil. For you, the planting of such seeds could be someone telling you, "I didn't like the way you said your speech," or "I expected more from you," or "Your sister was amazing at math, why are you struggling?" Judgement, unrealistic expectations, and comparison are all seeds that can create rotten roots that slowly alter your thinking, your creativity, and your confidence. When everything combines, it results in a paralyzing harvest of perfectionism.

This harvest brings doubt, rejection, fear, and shame right along with him. Not only does the harvest produce doubt in our abilities, but it also fuels doubt in God and His abilities. When this happens, you begin to question every single thing that you do and every single thought that you have, because you're afraid of the outcome.

When your identity, value, and happiness are tied to your achievements, you will live and die on the approval or disapproval of people.

Aside from being in bondage to the opinions of people, you will also find yourself in a perpetual cycle, thinking that the only thing you're worthy of producing is perfection. If you don't change, you will chase that until you die. I'm here to tell you that you will never be perfect. You will never produce perfection. It's impossible.

You're planted to produce results.

You're planted to produce transformations.

You're planted to produce witty ideas and inventions.

However, you're NOT planted to produce perfection.

Overcoming procrastination starts with setting realistic goals and taking imperfect action daily. Understanding that perfection is not an expectation God places on His children is one of the greatest revelations I've received.

In 1981, George T. Doran, a consultant and former director of corporate planning for Washington Water Power Company, published a paper called, "There's a S.M.A.R.T. Way to Write Management's Goals and Objectives." In the document, he introduces S.M.A.R.T. goals to the world as a tool to help others improve the chances of succeeding in accomplishing a goal.

S.M.A.R.T. is an acronym that stands for Specific. Measurable. Achievable. Relevant. Time Bound. Your goals should have each of these five elements.

Ensuring that my goals are S.M.A.R.T. allows me to combat my default behavior of setting unrealistic goals. As I work to accomplish my goals, particularly when I'm preparing to launch a new product or program to offer, I make the service or product available when I feel that I'm 80% complete.

The remaining 20% can be improved and finalized as I gather market research and client feedback. By setting both S.M.A.R.T. Goals and launching at 80%, I've gifted myself with so much grace and am slowly reprogramming my default settings.

I suggest that when you're 80% good, GO. When you're 80% there, GO. This is your new barometer for success. Try to reach the 80% threshold and share your products, programs, and service offerings with the world.

This new barometer doesn't come with a guarantee. Trust me, things won't work every time, however, you will accomplish more by setting healthy goals and making a habit to make imperfect action.

The problem with reaching success or launching a product or new offer when you've reached 100% is that "100%" is elusive. It's unrealistic and, by nature, an invitation to fall flat on your face.

Do not set a goal for yourself that by nature is designed for you to fail. The problem with perfectionism is that you create goals that were never meant for you to reach because they are so outlandish.

Don't you think it's time to give yourself grace? I'm talking about the kind of grace that comes in never-ending waves that continually wash over you daily. Grace that is there through every choice and all of the impact you'll have on this world.

People often go throughout life, bracing themselves for impact.

You're holding on while EXPECTING the worst to happen. You manifest destruction by your words and thoughts. You ASSUME you will be attacked.

You have thoughts such as:

- Someone's going to think I'm stupid.

- Someone's going to think I don't belong.

- I don't have what it takes to fix this issue.

This is where that imposter syndrome enters. You think you don't belong in a place that God sent you, yet every place you walk is Holy ground, every place you walk is your dominion. How can you not belong in the places that God sent you, but you feel like an imposter in your own land?

The enemy wants you to feel so small that everywhere you go and anytime you need to speak up, speak out, and produce, you don't; and the dreams die while inside of you, and then they shrivel up.

So you go through life, bracing yourself for impact while assuming something bad is going to happen. I'm here to propose a different way of experiencing life.

Instead of bracing yourself for impact, why don't you *grace yourself for impact*?

If you grace yourself for impact and for the things that God has called you to do, you will be as kind and loving to yourself as you are to everyone else.

If you brace yourself for impact and assume that your efforts will fail before you even try, you have already lost to self-sabotage. You'll set an unrealistic goal that you know you won't be able to meet, and then when you don't meet your goal, you will look at yourself like you're a horrible person when in reality you created a goal that was never designed to be experienced.

You made it impossible for you to reach it.

Grace yourself for impact.

You're assuming that you're going to do bad.

You're assuming that it's not going to work out.

You're assuming that you are going to fail.

If you grace yourself for the impact that you are designed to have on this world, you will do more than you ever thought you could do. You will reach more people than you ever thought you could reach and obtain joy and peace that passes all understanding while doing it.

Grace yourself for impact, don't brace yourself for impact.

Grace yourself, and do not believe that because God is showing you greater that He is being cruel to you.

He is showing you, you in the future.

He is showing you how He sees you in his mind's eye so that you can hold on and survive your season of being planted, not buried.

You have too much inside of you not to produce.

Chapter 2

Rooted

"Let your roots grow down into him, and let your lives be built on him. Then your faith will grow strong in the truth you were taught, and you will overflow with thankfulness." - Colossians 2:7

Do not despise these small beginnings, for the Lord rejoices to see the work begin, to see the plumb line in Zerubbabel's hand. - Zechariah 4:10 (NLT)

If you are planted right now and you are not sure when your roots will grow, I want to encourage you not to despise the day of small beginnings. Do not despise where you are right now. If you are working at a grocery store, bagging groceries, or if you're a temp worker at an agency (like I used to be) while also building your business, do not despise your current season.

Do not look at where you're planted right now and get discouraged because I can assure you, the very thing that you're ashamed of and that you want to hide from the world is the exact thing that God is going to use to secure your foundation.

Your present season is going to develop your roots and ensure that you're stable for your next level. The struggle that you're experiencing and enduring right now, along with the corresponding shame that may be attacking you, is not what God sees when He shines His face upon you. In your season of being planted, God is building maturity in you and he wants to bring you into the fullness of who you are by growing your roots deeper in Him.

Your *rooted* season is quite possibly one of the most important seasons in your journey. When you are rooted, you will either shift closer to God or further away from God's dream for you. Your rooted season will draw people closer to Christ or make them run far away from Him. Your rooted season will also draw people closer to you, for this season is where your underdog story is being written. This shift to growing roots will bring clients to you, and bring friends that are equally yoked to you.

When I started my law firm, my husband turned half of my walk-in closet into an office. I affectionately call it my "cloffice." (Get it? Closet + Office = Cloffice. I digress.) I still work there from time to time if I'm working from home. Honestly, that closet is where my roots were established as an entrepreneur.

A couple of years into my business, Facebook contacted me and offered to shoot a documentary-style video of my law firm. They wanted to see where I worked and what I did on a day-to-day.

I was so excited! Then shame set in. The cloffice I loved and adored suddenly became too small for Facebook. Even with my success and being recognized by a major company, something in me was telling me that my space still wasn't good enough.

Something was saying, "Ticora you have to show them you're bigger. The closet isn't acceptable. It's no longer good enough."

I began to look for places in my home to dress up a bit more to be more acceptable for a Facebook feature. I stopped myself while lugging my ring light out and setting it up in my family room.

This. Isn't. Me.

I get on my knees and pray in that closet. I meditate in that closet. I've paced in circles during client calls there. I built my business there.

I've cried there.

I've moved sticky notes on my kanban board in that closet.

I'm a boss in that closet.

It's what people need to see. I'm not going to hide who I am. I don't need to be ashamed of where my roots are.

If I start filtering my life like some Instagram post, I'll continue to do that until I become a shell of my former self.

So, I lugged all of my stuff back into my cloffice. The video team at Facebook arrived at my home and I showed them where I worked.

They LOVED it!

They loved every part of my story, including my cloffice. Everything that looked like it would disqualify me QUALIFIED me for that opportunity. In the end, what mattered was my authentic story, and not the filtered version I was attempting to create.

None of the things I thought mattered made a difference in the end because God was knitting my story together, even the unpretty parts, for my good. Just like you. God is knitting the story of your rooted season together so that it will be used in a way to make your name and His name great.

The things that you think are a curse upon you are not. God sees you in your rooted season. He has not forgotten about you in your place of growth.

He sees the hard work that you're putting in. He sees your heart. He sees the midnight hour and what you're doing as darkness surrounds you. He sees you staying up late. He sees you rising early. And, He also sees if you're not spending time with him.

Making your dream an idol will rot your roots. Do not let this season consume your every thought while you neglect the One who gave you your dream. Avoid neglecting your family and friends during this process. Trust me, God knows the desires of your heart, and He is going to bring forth everything in accordance to the right season.

One of my favorite scriptures is Philippians 1:6 and it says, "He who started a good work in you, will carry it out to completion until the day of Christ Jesus."

The good works that are starting in you right now God is going to do His part to make sure they are complete. If your roots take hold firmly in Him, you will finish the good work, however, if you do not someone else will be called to complete the task, because you did not obey.

Don't Resist Your Roots

It is a guarantee that in your rooted season you will face attacks, obstacles, and challenges from many angles. These attacks may come in many forms; however, in my experience, doubt, indecision, and procrastination are the strongest attacks as they primarily occur within your mind. Despite knowing God's promises, many of us allow what God boldly plants inside us to be uprooted with ease.

To uproot means to "pull out of the ground; dig up or move someone from their home or a familiar location." For you, this may look like running from one career to the next because your boss corrected you. It may also look like abandoning a business idea because you didn't reach six-figures in sixty days. More often, we allow our God ideas to be dug up when a friend (or foe) tells us our God ideas aren't going to work out.

These challenges are to be expected when we're on a God-ordained path. They come to test how firmly rooted and committed you are to what God planted in you.

Why should God trust you to steward His amazing plans for your life if you're going to dig up everything He planted in you? You need to prove that you can be trusted to manage and execute His plans before He can reward you with greater.

He is searching for sons and daughters who have faith in Him. Faith personified is looking your naysayers in the face when they challenge the God in you and replying, "I trust God. I trust His plans. I won't fail."

Faith is not justifying your choices.

Faith is not explaining the rationale behind your decisions.

Faith is not knowing every single step to take.

Faith is trusting that God will work everything out.

Faith is pressing forward towards the promise.

Faith is enduring your rooted season while knowing that one day you will break through the darkness and *emerge* in due time.

You have to press forth through the darkness and mud in which you've been planted in order to fight your way to the surface, all while simultaneously rooting yourself deeper and deeper in God's ground.

Being rooted develops you as a problem solver, an invaluable strategist, a fighter, and a creative. As you grow deeper in Christ, you mature, you trust, you obey, and you become free.

What I remember the most about my rooted season are the attacks I experienced. I was convinced that I was stupid, inadequate, incompetent, and not worthy to pursue the dreams God planted inside of me. I was convinced that even if I did pursue the call on my life, I wouldn't be able to sustain what I wanted to build since I had failed so many times before. I didn't go to the best law school or graduate with a stellar gpa. I was looking at everything this world deems unfavorable and imperfect as a disqualification for my dreams.

If we do not uproot unhealthy mindsets of unworthiness, we will carry toxicity with us into our next seasons. We will convince ourselves that we are buried only to be forgotten, not planted to be fruitful.

The purpose of your rooted season is twofold: to dig deep and to dig out. You must dig deeper into God's Word, His plans, and His purpose for you, while also digging out everything in you that is not of God. The same mindset that got you into the ground will not get you out of the ground.

We cannot bring the mindset of shame, lack, and unworthiness to the surface, because it will sink you. Neither can you resist the process of being rooted. You were planted to produce, not planted to reduce. Embrace this season and the struggle that comes with it.

Praise God for the opportunity to dig deeper in Him and dig out what is not like Him, because once you emerge, you're going to understand why your trials came. Again, those same trials will be used to QUALIFY you, not disqualify you.

Visit www.ticoradavis.com/resources to view the mini-documentary shot by Facebook and other resources to strengthen your roots.

Chapter 3

Emergence

"A shoot will [emerge] from the stump of Jesse; from his roots a Branch will bear fruit." - Isaiah 11:1 (NIV)

A dormant seed will come to life if you add water and plant it in an optimal environment. Doing this will transform the seed from a state of being inactive to active. To thrive, roots will spring forth and travel in search of water. The farther they travel, the more they anchor the plant to its foundation. As the roots expand their search, they deliver water and nutrients from the soil back to the plant.

All of this amazing work of anchoring, searching, finding, and nurturing is going on beneath the surface, unseen by the human eye, to stabilize the plant's foundation. Like a seed coming alive, change for us always begins deep beneath the surface to take us from a state of inactivity to activity, from stagnation to starting, from procrastination to acceleration, from disorientation to revelation.

Being rooted is such a precious season for you when you are covered by God to facilitate a cure for your confusion and heartbreak. Eventually, you will be required to either emerge and break through the soil you're planted in or rot in the ground.

I received this revelation when I visited my parent's home, my childhood home, after a terrible fire. Almost everything in the house was destroyed by either fire, smoke, or water damage. The floors, walls, and room were all ripped out. The only thing existing from the original structure was the frame of the home and my mother's sunroom.

Rebuilding the home has taken almost a year and I've personally experienced a succession of losses since our home caught fire. Not only did I lose the house, but I lost my great grandmother, a close friend and my daddy. Nothing is the same since the fire, and all of this came to a head as I returned to see the progress the builders were making.

Have you ever been in a place and said to yourself, "Wow, this is the exact same place that it always was, but it looks completely different on the inside?"

There are new floors, new fixtures, new doors, and a new kitchen. Everything is new and different. Now, don't get me wrong, the work they've done is beautiful, but the house is not the same.

As I observed the new changes, I thought, "Wow, this is not the same house." Of course, it's the same place on the outside, but on the inside everything has been completely redone.

This revelation made me think of a prophetic word I received from my Apostle that I was led to share on a Facebook status. I shared her words which, in summary, were: "Ticora, You're going to be anointed to speak over people creatively. You are going to have the power to birth creativity in people with your words."

Upon sharing that status, I received inbox messages and comments underneath the post requesting that I speak into their lives. It seemed as if their roots were hungry for an encouraging word to nourish their souls.

The multiple requests to "Speak into my life, Ticora" made me see how desperate people are for validation in their rooted season. When you're rooted, you're often tired of being in the dark and unsure of your next steps. You're ready to move to higher ground, but you're afraid to activate what was always inside of you.

So, you attempt to rebuild your inner structure with someone else's words. I'm sure that you've been guilty of waiting on someone to share their thoughts and opinions with you about your life and what your next steps should be. Perhaps you've even gotten frustrated with people for not telling you what to do, or empathizing with your current place spiritually.

I'm here to tell you that nobody is obligated to speak life into your life. You already have what you need to change your situation. Like my parents' home that was structurally the same but internally changed, you too have the power to demolish, rebuild, and refine your present situation.

The Word of God is already in you. The power to emerge is already in you.

To 'emerge' is defined as to "move out of or away from something and come into view."

I'm here to tell you that you don't need permission from external things or people to come into view of the world. You no longer need to wait for permission to come out of hiding. You can give your own self permission.

There's no need to look for someone to speak over you or say something to inspire you to emerge.

The emergence is already in you.

You don't need me or anybody else to tell you that you're ready, that you're talented, or that your ideas are amazing. You have to be able to encourage yourself and give yourself permission to move out of the ground and to the surface.

God has already spoken to you through your visions and dreams for your own life. You know what you're supposed to do, however, you're waiting for someone to validate and approve your ideas before you have the confidence to pursue them. When you fail to receive validation, you use that as an excuse to procrastinate.

That is at the heart of why you're seeking third-party validation.

You are seeking someone to validate your ideas, your existence, and your dreams because for some reason, you cannot self-validate. And in turn, you procrastinate, which is really being disobedient, and you are turning your back on all the people that are waiting on the other side of your obedience. There are people who are assigned to your dreams, to your books, your ideas,your visions, and to your business. People are assigned and they are waiting for you to emerge and transform their lives with your products, programs and service offerings. The word that you are waiting on to validate your emergence is already inside of you. Every single thing that you're looking to this world to provide, you already have it.

You have every single thing in you that the people on top have. You don't need another prophetic word. You don't need somebody else to speak over you. You don't need anybody else to validate it.

You don't need any more confirmation.

What you need is discipline and obedience. You are destined to emerge in pursuit of your your dreams, but you will be required to activate faith for it to happen.

To be clear, you need to activate full faith in God. If you are struggling with procrastination, if you are struggling with fear and shame, all of those struggles take their roots in a lack of faith. It is a lack of faith that makes you grapple with the thoughts of "Can I do it again? Do I have what it takes? Do I really belong here?"

This busy battle of the mind results in an overloaded brain and paralysis of our purpose. Procrastination always shows up when we overthink.

Which is why you have to work your faith like a muscle. Now, I'm not telling you to train your faith muscle as if you're preparing for a triathlon, but you do need to do a few crunches and push-ups on a daily basis.

As you gradually grow stronger in faith, you will be able to encourage yourself instead of seeking encouragement and confirmation from others.

Again, like I said, you don't need any more confirmation. You don't need another great sermon. You need to be obedient and pursue what it is that God has called you to do.

As believers, we need deliverance from indecision and stagnation. We have the power to be delivered from overthinking ourselves into a state of stuckness. The more you realize your power, the faster you will progress. You may even think, "This business plan *on paper* looks like a bad idea."

On paper, it doesn't look like I should've started a law firm. On paper, it looks like I should've just played the safe route and continued to work contract jobs until a cushy corporate lawyer gig found me. At least when I was making $20 an hour as a contract attorney, I knew I could depend on a new temp job every 2 weeks. My struggle was a reliable one. The "entrepreneurial struggle" would be wrought with unexpected and uncalculated highs and lows. As a contract attorney, I didn't need to have faith, because I knew what to expect.

Success didn't look very promising when I launched my law firm with a seven-month old baby on my hip. Nor did sustaining an intellectual property law firm seem to be within reach when I had only filed two trademark applications before opening my doors. I've learned that what it *looks like* is rarely what it's *lived out like* when you operate in faith.

Recently, after two and a half years of being in business, I filed my 260th trademark application. I've come a long way from the two I started with.

Having mustard seed-sized faith empowered me to validate my dreams, activate my purpose and emerge into the marketplace. What I love about "mustard seed faith" is that you aren't required to have excessive faith. Your faith can barely exist and it will be enough for God to work a miracle with as long you're willing to do the work to emerge.

Visit www.ticoradavis.com/resources for resources to help you emerge.

Chapter 4

Stagnation

Abide in me, and I in you. As the branch cannot bear fruit by itself, unless it abides in the vine, neither can you, unless you abide in me. - John 15:4

Enlarge the place of your tent, stretch your tent curtains wide, do not hold back; lengthen your cords, strengthen your stakes. For you will spread out to the right and to the left; your descendants will dispossess nations and settle in their desolate cities.
- Isaiah 54:2-3

One Sunday my Apostle Gary Bellinger preached on the subject of being on time. As someone who has struggled with punctuality, I knew I needed to pay close attention to this sermon. I assumed this would be a typical message about stewardship over our time or honoring leadership, but I was pleasantly mistaken.

Apostle Bellinger shared that the devil doesn't necessarily want to stop us from getting to the place where God wants us to be (ultimately, the will of God is going to happen for your life if you submit). He shared that the enemy wants to *delay* our arrival. In delaying our arrival, we won't be able to experience the fullness of the moment nor the fullness of God.

For example, let's say you arrive at a destination 15 minutes late. Big deal, right? You're still there and you likely didn't miss much of the function. In your mind, what's important is that you've made it to the event, albeit a few minutes late. However, because you were late, you didn't get the full experience. Even if you were 5 minutes late, you still missed 300 seconds of the event.

I want you to consider the moments in your life where you showed up late to class, late to work, or late to an event. Perhaps your delayed arrival resulted in you missing out on important details about an extra credit opportunity, the opportunity to travel on the company's dime, or the opportunity to meet and bond with other business owners. Those seconds you missed due to your tardiness may have cost you resources, rewards, and relationships.

When it comes to being late for stepping into your destiny, it may cost you even more.

Guy Raz hosts the NPR podcast *How I Built This?* Guy interviews the most successful business owners in the world to discover the stories, ideas and movements behind their iconic brands. I noticed that in almost every episode he asks his guests whether luck played a role in their success. Their answers are as diverse as their businesses. As I listened to numerous episodes, I noticed a common thread amongst their answers.

Here are a few responses I gathered from Guy's question about luck:

1. "I have this thesis that the world runs on luck, the question is what you do with it. Everyone gets lucky for some amount in their life and the question is are you alert enough to know you're being lucky or you're becoming lucky? Are you talented enough to take that advantage and run with it and do you have enough grit, do you have enough resilience to stay with it when it gets hard?" – *Kevin Systrom & Mike Krieger, Instagram*

2. "You know what being lucky means? It means having the skill to grab the luck when it's presented to you." – *Haim Saban, Power Rangers*

3. "To be a billionaire you've gotta get lucky. I started my company at a time when the stock market was going nuts, and that was my luck. I was smart enough to do it, smart enough to run it, smart enough to execute on it, smart enough to hedge it. But, no question there was luck involved." – *Mark Cuban, Serial Entrepreneur*

4. "We like to say that there's a lot of deliberate serendipity. For example, we were really lucky to be exposed to our marketing professor who helped us think through

pricing. But we had created goodwill by being friendly and doing well in his class, that he was willing to dedicate time to us." – *Dave Gilboa & Neil Blumenthal, Warby Parker*

5. "I really don't believe in luck. I believe that the reason we're still here is the perseverance. To the extent there is luck, it's the timing the way the consumers evolved but I've heard something when someone says, oh you know you were in the right place at the right time. I said, well you know, it took ten years to get to that right place. So this wasn't something that just happened overnight." – *Seth Goldman, Honest Tea*

6. "There's no luck. I don't really believe in luck. This has been very hard. There were a lot of days I didn't think that I would keep this business. I think part of it is drive and I saw where we needed to go, giving up was not an option." – *Kendra Scott, Kendra Scott Jewelry*

7. "I do believe in luck. I've had many, many, many lucky breaks, including meeting Ramon at the diner that night, right? That was the beginning. Or the very good luck of having my parents as parents – not bad, right? Once you grow up, you make your own luck. Definitely you make your own luck. I think all the lucky breaks I had were more a result of me staying in the game and just believing something would break, just hanging around long enough. That's more important than luck in my opinion, being aggressive at every opportunity

and standing up for yourself – yes, more important than luck." – *Barbara Corcoran, The Corcoran Group*

8. "I think luck only happens when you are actively moving and searching for what is next. Start moving. Look for the horizon." – *Jose Andres, Celebrity Chef*

Luck is defined as "success or failure apparently brought by chance rather than through one's own actions."

Whether you believe in luck or not, you cannot dispute the fact that each of these moguls shifted into success because they positioned themselves to do so. They were not stagnant. They were searching, moving and taking action to find solutions to common problems. As a result, they found themselves in the right place at the right time prepared to produce greatness.

Choosing to be stagnant, late and ill prepared for your next opportunity will cause critical delays, missed opportunities, and someone else getting the glory for your amazing ideas. How many times have you seen a commercial with a new gizmo or gadget that you conceived of years prior, but never took action to pursue? Too many to count I'm sure.

When I look back over my life and remember moments of growth and revelation, I was always in a position to receive my breakthrough. I positioned myself by seeking healing, therapy, wisdom, knowledge, and understanding to combat my life's challenges.

As I remember my Apostle's words and the testimonies of those millionaires, I realize that being in position isn't enough if I get ready two years too late.

I ask, "God, what have I missed when I arrive to church late? When I arrive to networking events late? When I delay implementing transitions in my business, what am I missing out on?"

I dug deeper and asked, "Who is missing out on the transformation I have to offer, because I am delaying my arrival?"

What is the cost of my stagnation? To be stagnant means you are dull, sluggish and show little to no activity. Stagnation is further defined as "having no current or flow and often having an unpleasant smell as a consequence."

When plants experience stagnation, the water in the soil sits too long without being taken up by the plant's roots. When water stagnates, mold and mildew set in, often resulting in rotting the roots of the plant. Stagnation often occurs in indoor plants when one fails to move the plant to a bigger pot (i.e., a larger growth environment.)

The process of stagnation is procrastination personified. You attend conferences, purchase courses, and join communities to obtain the knowledge you need to pursue your dreams. With all the knowledge you gain, you fail to implement because you either feel you're not ready or you feel you need to do more research before you feel ready. Overthinking and fear of the unknown render you paralyzed, unable to move from the place you're in to the place you need to be.

There's a cost that comes with choosing to stay stuck. The fresh ideas God gives you in one season can become outdated and stale in the next, all because you failed to step out on faith and implement what you've learned quickly. I truly believe procrastination has caused me to miss million-dollar moments. Now, this doesn't mean that God won't provide or ensure I'm successful; however, it can mean that my failure to move at the right time could result in me missing out on the fullness of God's best for me.

I personally experienced the power of obeying God and stepping into my calling, even when I didn't feel ready, in December 2016. At this time, I had finally made the decision to open my law firm. My plan was to open the firm in August 2017. It seemed like a perfectly wise plan as my son would be one year old at the time, I would've had more time to obtain training in the area of creative business law, which was my desired focus, and save money to start a new business.

At church, Apostle Bellinger called me up the front and began to share a prophetic word for my life. He said:

> "Ticora, God says to make haste. Open your law firm as fast as you can. God will send you clients from all over the country and all over the world. The time is now for you to move...
>
> You will not fail."

I listened and stepped into agreement with the prophetic word. Although I felt as if I was moving months ahead of my initial plan, that day I made steps to open my law firm by submitting the proper paperwork. We opened the virtual doors to The Creator's Law Firm on January 16, 2017.

On January 20, 2017 I received a phone call from television producers from VH1 to see whether I was interested in appearing on one of their reality tv shows.

I had a plan, but God had a promise.

Sometimes I consider how different things would've been if I decided to pursue my initial plan of opening my firm in August as opposed to January as the Lord instructed. What would my stagnation have cost me? I certainly would've missed the VH1 opportunity which opened so many doors for me.

I would've also missed the knowledge I gained from my first clients, the connections I created with other businesses, and meeting lifelong friends. Like a plant whose root growth has slowed due to their cramped environment, refusing to move from your present situation to the next will stagnate your growth. Not only will you miss opportunities, you'll also miss connections.

Even worse, not moving at all may kill your dreams. Potted plants become root bound when they outgrow their present container and aren't repotted in a larger one. Their roots grow round and round, until their growth is stunted. In essence, the roots choke the life out of the plant resulting in its death.

Stagnation has little to do with being lazy. A lot of people think that if you're a procrastinator, you're lazy. When I began to study scriptures on procrastination, I read everything the Bible had to say about "laziness."

I read scriptures such as:

> *Lazy hands make for poverty, but diligent hands bring wealth. - Proverbs 10:4*

> *A sluggard buries his hand in the dish; he is too lazy to bring it back to his mouth. - Proverbs 26:15*

> *How long will you lie there, you sluggard? When will you get up from your sleep? A little sleep, a little slumber, a little folding of the hands to rest— and poverty will come on you like a thief and scarcity like an armed man. - Proverbs 6:9-11*

As a result, I would condemn myself and feel absolutely terrible. I would even talk to myself negatively and say, "You're lazy. You're a sluggard. You're going to end up in poverty."

I was cursing myself because I was too immature to realize the cause of my troubles.

Being stuck doesn't mean you're lazy; however, it likely means you lack revelation. When revelation comes, you THEN have two choices:

(1) To move, or

(2) have God move on.

Through studying the psychology of procrastination, it was revealed to me that procrastinators are not lazy or lack motivation. In fact, those suffering from procrastination are very motivated to have a different life and new set of behaviors. Procrastinators suffer from perfectionism, imposter syndrome, and anxiety, amongst other things.

My studies revealed that the root of my personal procrastination problem was anxiety.

For me, anxiety shows up when I'm faced with a task that I feel is challenging. Even if I've successfully completed similar tasks in the past, my anxiety convinces me that perhaps the last time I overcame an obstacle was a fluke, and I won't be able to replicate my success a second time.

This is what happens to those of us who have outgrown our pots and are being ushered to produce the greatness inside of us. Delaying the pursuit of our God-sized dreams because we think the dream is too big to achieve, and even questioning whether or not we can sustain the vision will cause us to arrive at our destination later than God intended.

I don't want you to become bound by your refusal to move from your current environment to a larger territory. This is exactly what happens when you allow fear to keep you stuck. Failing to pursue your next level, whether that be higher education, a new business, or leaving your dead end job, will have you running in circles, just like those roots in the pot that's too small. You will overthink, question your calling, and second guess God, when you all you really need to do is uproot yourself.

I don't know about you, but I want to experience everything God has for me.

The fullness of God won't be found in your comfort zone (or pot). However, it will be found in your next level as you allow your roots to stretch out and collect new experiences to mature you in Christ.

If you've gotten this far in the book, it's likely because you're ready to expand. The choice is yours. You can put this book down and make zero changes in your life by staying stuck in your pot, or you can choose to move to your next level and allow your roots to expand all around you.

The fullness of God is in your expansion.

Now, move.

⌒

Visit www.ticoradavis.com/resources for resources to help you get unstuck.

Chapter 5

Expansion

"The best way to predict your future is to create it." -
Abraham Lincoln

A s we prepare to move out of our comfort zones, we must be bold in what God has called us to do. Boldness is defined as "not hesitating or fearful in the face of possible danger." In short, it means being courageous.

You cannot be coy, shy, or bashful when you move out of your pot. What happens when you are unapologetically confident in God's plan for your life is that you are going to make other people who are still stuck in their pots even more uncomfortable than they already are.

Folks who are in their dormant stage may criticize your choice to expand. If you are rooted, their criticism should not move you back to your comfort zone. When you're planted to produce, you don't shrink back.

What I want you to be aware of is that when you are pursuing your dreams, when you begin to walk boldly and hit your stride, expect pushback. It's going to happen, because external and internal forces are designed to stagnate your expansion.

Challenges may present themselves as individuals taking issue with your unique business choices or your internal voice of doubt. By design, these seeds of doubt are planted to make you timid.

Doubt is designed to make you lack confidence in God's calling on your life. Doubt is designed to make you delay pursuing your God-sized dreams. It's designed to plant a seed of fear in you so that the next time you take steps towards expansion, you overthink. You second guess. You procrastinate. Doubt is designed to delay your destiny.

When people challenge your choices, oppose your platform, and attempt to mischaracterize your efforts, they are testing whether you will shrink back.

In short, the trials are a test of your timidity. The definition of timidity is *showing a lack of courage, a lack of confidence, or to be easily frightened.*

What does it mean to be easily frightened?

To be timid means that someone doesn't have to make much effort to make you afraid.

Satan's desire is for you to be so easily frightened that you stay bound in your comfort zone and take no action at all.

Your naysayers who may publicly or privately criticize your choices want you to sit in your house and have you over-think everything you do in connection with your purpose. If you have thoughts such as, "I'm not ready," or "Today isn't the best to send an email sharing my new offer," or "Now, isn't the right time to launch. I'm going to sit on this idea for another three months or another three years,"... that's timid-ity at play.

External resistance may come from family, friends, or follow-ers. Resistance from familiar faces shouldn't surprise you, be-cause change always makes people uncomfortable. Your choice to expand will hold a mirror of accountability up to the faces of those closest to you and reflect the lack of action they're taking in their own lives.

Sometimes pushback comes from folks behind internet screens. I recorded a Facebook live video entitled "Being Timid is Kill-ing Your Business." I was inspired to record the video after fac-ing criticism from a stranger. After conversing with this indi-vidual, my boldness for my business and desire to encourage others began to shrink.

I literally felt myself walking on eggshells. I began to hesitate before posting a status on social media, following up with a cli-ent, or working on my book. Based on a single interaction with ONE person, my mental behavior changed.

I shared this with my husband and he powerfully encouraged me. Passionately, he told me, "Ticora, it's your platform. This is YOUR purpose, Ticora. You CANNOT be timid about your purpose. I won't have it."

Criticism comes with the territory of entrepreneurship. Whether it's from your clients or customers, your friends or family, or from yourself, t's one of life's guarantees, along with taxes and death.

What does not have to be a guarantee is the type of fear that often accompanies criticism. The fear that breeds timidity and the inclination to shrink from your purpose.

To quote my better whole, "You CANNOT be timid about your purpose."

So, I'll say it again...a little differently this time.

You cannot be EASILY FRIGHTENED about your purpose.

To be "easily frightened" means that small people and small encounters can cause all of the momentum you've built up to slow down, become stagnant and eventually stop.

To be "easily frightened" means that you show up late or not at all.

To be "easily frightened" means you talk yourself out of God-ideas.

To be "easily frightened" means that someone has to make very little effort to cause you to tremble.

Nobody wants to listen to shy people or people who are timid. Nobody wants to purchase from them either. You have to be unapologetic. Not offensive, not rude, not mean, but BOLD about who God has called you to be and what He has called you do in your life and business.

Do not be easily frightened in this season, because your purpose, your destiny, and the people assigned to your life, your calling, and your next chapter need you expand now.

Fear's Purpose is to Shock You

Fear, in and of itself, honestly is not a bad thing. Fear's entire purpose is to keep us safe. Being afraid to drive 100 miles per hour in a 30 miles per hour zone will prevent you from getting a speeding ticket, losing your license, or having a horrific car accident. Fear is pretty useful in this situation.

When fear is misplaced and not put in the appropriate position, it shocks you back to your safe zone.

Fear kept me in a depression for five years.

Fear convinced me that I was stupid.

Fear tricked me into thinking no one would love me.

Fear made me think that I couldn't have a family of my own one day or become successful.

Fear convinced me that I was somebody else that I wasn't.

And not only did fear convince me that I was a stranger to myself, it convinced me that I didn't have the power within to build a life I would love. I was duped into believing that I was unworthy of the opportunities that came to me so I should settle where I was, because it was what I had always known. Fear was reliable, fear was consistent, and fear was safe.

Although I can appreciate the reliability of fear, especially in an unreliable world, I was not growing any closer to the vision God had for my life.

Growth happens outside your safe zone.

Knowing that growth would require courage, I sought solutions. At this time, I received the revelation of the distinct relationship between fear and courage.

Author and podcaster Michael Hyatt stated that, "Courage is the willingness to act in spite of your fear."

In "The Big Leap", Gay Hendricks shares a dynamic quote from George S. Patton that truly summarizes the synergistic relationship between courage and fear. Patton states, "Courage is fear holding on a minute longer."

For years, I lived in fear without realizing that I was closer than I thought to activating courage.

Hendricks shares that the same neurological processes and the same emotions that cause fear also cause courage. The difference with courage is that you keep holding on, and you push past the fear that paralyzes you, step out on faith, and do the things that scare you.

Think of every time you've mustered up the courage to do something you were afraid to do. Think of the courage that it took for you to say 'Okay, I'm publishing my Facebook business page, launching my business, and pitching myself for a speaking engagement.'

Prior to taking that leap, you were likely a little fearful to publish the page, send an email, or share that you're a new business owner. Despite those fears, you held on, proceeded, and activated courage. Those are the moments you beat fear.

Now, those moments you experience may be fleeting, but you did it.

If you're anything like me, the moments you activated courage may be major life events you've discounted. When you look at your past actions and say *"You know what, that wasn't that big of a deal,"* you're not acknowledging your power and your shifts.

Even if you feel like you aren't courageous or bold or strong or even capable, your past actions prove otherwise.

So, the next time fear comes up for you, remember to just push past it and hold on. Don't get into a battle with fear. Don't go back and forth in your mind about whether or not you should or shouldn't do something, and wonder whether or not someone is going to judge you.

People are going to judge you, and people are not going to like you. People are going to have a problem with you walking in your purpose. Their discomfort is not your concern.

You pursuing what God has called you to do has nothing to do with anyone else. Don't allow anyone to make you feel that your obedience to God is an offense to them. If someone is offended by you walking in your purpose, that is a personal problem that has to do with themselves.

If you're allowing your next steps to be manipulated by every comment, every naysayer, and the things people say about you, check your roots. You may need to dig deeper in God, remind yourself of the greatness inside of you, and activate courage.

Courage is boldness personified. Courage is saying you're going to do it anyway despite what everybody else thinks.

I'm not saying you're going to demolish and crush fear every time it presents itself.

In fact, the bad news is that fear is going to try to shock you into safety. The good news is you get to put fear in its place even if it tags along.

You and you alone are in control of your journey. When you beat fear, you are choosing to push past the safety and shock to plant your roots in new ground.

When plants are uprooted they sometimes experience a phenomenon called "transplant shock." Plant shock or transplant shock occurs most often in outdoor plants that are uprooted and planted in new soil.

Some plants die while being uprooted, while others flourish. When moving a plant, the best chance of survival occurs when you disturb the roots of the plant as little as possible, bring as much of the roots with you as possible, and water thoroughly after transplanting.

Moving away from your pot and expanding your roots is going to be uncomfortable, but is required in order for you to produce. As you prepare to activate courage remember not to disturb your roots and relationship with God, bring all of God with you on the journey and wwashater yourself with His word after transplanting yourself to new ground.

You cannot produce what's inside of you by staying stuck in one place. Nor, can you produce a bountiful harvest by running back to your safe zone (or pot).

Do not be timid, because your rethinking, overthinking, and refusal to take significant action is preventing your expansion. Your delay is grieving your purpose. Your disobedience is hurting your pocketbook, but most of all, it's hurting the people that are assigned to your life now, and to your next chapter.

To watch my Facebook live, visit: ticoradavis.com/resources

Chapter 6

Focused Faith

"Concentrate all your thoughts upon the work at hand. The sun's rays do not burn until brought to a focus." - Alexander Graham Bell

If you want to accomplish your goals, two things will be required of you:

Focus and faith.

You need to have faith in yourself and you need to have faith in God. In addition to faith, you need to develop the habit of focus.

If you're at a standstill in your life or business, it's likely not because your business isn't operating well or you have bad luck. It's most likely due to the fact that you haven't focused on one thing long enough to develop a modicum of expertise.

Abandoning processes, systems, programs, products and offers when you face roadblocks and challenges is not being innovative, it's being elusive. It's running away from your problems instead of viewing them as an opportunity for growth and development.

Challenges come so that we can grow. In the book of James it says, "Consider it pure joy, my brothers, when you face trials of many kinds, because those trials will allow you to develop perseverance. And perseverance must finish its work so you can be mature, complete, and not lacking anything."

That is why when trials come your way, whether it be in your business, marriage, etc ,it is something that you should have pure joy about. You should be thankful for the challenge because there is an unfinished work in your heart. There's an unfinished work in your mind. There's an unfinished work in your business, so that means that you're constantly in a state of improving.

Encountering trials means that you can always go to another level, and that you can serve more people. It means that your heart can be enlarged and your territory can be expanded. Facing trials does not mean that you've veered off your purpose path. When you face a trial, that is an opportunity for you to grow, and if you continue to face the same trial, it's likely because you have yet to pass the test.

You are not a mistake. You are here on purpose. You have a calling, an anointing, and there is something that only you can do, and you have been called to do it. It doesn't matter if somebody else has the same title, or if they attended the same school. It doesn't matter if somebody even shares some of your DNA. At the end of the day, you are anointed to produce what God has put inside of you. That means that you have to focus and you have to have faith to achieve your calling. If you have one or the other, it's not going to work.

You can have faith, but faith without works is dead. For example, you can have faith that something's going to happen, but if you put absolutely zero work behind it, nothing is going to come to you. Alternatively, if you only have focus, you could be focused on the wrong thing. You could be so focused on one aspect of your problem that it fails to do anything to help you produce a harvest.

We have to have a focused faith. When you focus, that means you Follow One Course Until Success. Faith is the substance of what's hoped for, the evidence of things not seen. So if you follow one course until you are successful, and you have faith in the course that you are following, I guarantee you that it's going to work out for your good.

What I love about this journey is that you don't have to have a lot of faith for things to work out. If you have faith the size of a mustard seed, that is all that is required. A mustard seed is smaller than a grain of sand.

The effort of faith you have to put forth is tiny. With faith and focus, you will have a winning combination.

When your faith is activated, you must ensure that you don't allow anything to rob you of the faith you do have. Oftentimes, this is what happens when someone loses their faith.

Your tiny faith is snatched up at the first sight of opposition.

You have faith, and then you turn around and you allow yourself to be robbed of it. You allow it to be snatched away from quickly. In turn, you are convinced that you need BIG faith for it to stick around. Again, BIG faith is not required. All you need is a tiny faith to be an overcomer.

My dear friend Ty Jackson (@tyspeaks) taught me that we have the anointing as our advantage as kingdom entrepreneurs. We have such an advantage on our side because we have God. As long as you want to stay in agreement with God, you're always going to be in the majority. That's why favor keeps coming down, and favor keeps shining on people's businesses because in spite of what is happening, in spite of the obstacles, they go for it anyway. Even if they don't feel completely and totally competent in the path forward, they pursue it, they move forward, and they go for it anyway. They don't allow anything to stop them.

Remember this when you receive unsolicited feedback. I recall when applying to law school, there was a man who worked for the university whose job was to assist students with applying to graduate schools. I scheduled an appointment with him to find out what I needed to do to go to law school.

During my appointment, I requested the necessary information regarding the exams I needed to take and the admission requirements.

I scheduled the appointment, knowing I had poor grades and a terrible G.P.A. In short, on paper, I didn't look like a budding future lawyer.

So I said to this man, "I need to know how to get into law school. Please provide me with the information." And he kept saying, "Well, it's going to be really difficult for you to get in... you know your GPA is really low, and it's going to be difficult for you."

I just looked at him and I said, "I'm very well aware of what my GPA is. I have it, it's mine. I'm privy to that information. You're not telling me anything that I didn't know. I would like for us to focus this meeting on the steps that I need to take to get into school."

For many of you reading this book, you may look at your accomplishments, or lack thereof, and conclude that "on paper" things don't look very promising. You judge yourself about your past mistakes so you don't even give yourself one second to dream or consider that circumstances could be better...you don't give yourself one second to think that you can overcome. Even worse, you listen to what other people say and allow them to define your destiny.

With focused faith, you can shut down any opposition. I refuse to allow anyone to plant seeds of doubt and destruction into my destiny. I'm not going to allow anyone to tell me what I can and cannot do. You cannot convince me that a challenge is going to be hard for me and expect me to accept your word at face value.

My faith and my focus state otherwise.

Chapter 7

Sow

"Success is... knowing your purpose in life, growing to reach your maximum potential, and sowing seeds that benefit others." - John C. Maxwell

In 2015, my husband, Tyrone, and I discovered that we would become parents for the first time. Our hearts and my belly were filled with promise, joy, and disbelief at the idea that we somehow were chosen to welcome this new life into the world. We navigated the common doubts and fears facing many first time parents and questioned whether we would be *good enough* to raise our son, Miles.

The anticipation of welcoming a child brought out intense discussions between Ty and I that we'd *never* had before. We shared so many opposing views as to how we would raise Miles. We discussed the most important things, such as:

- Cloth diapers or disposables

- Home school or daycare

- Veggies or chicken nuggets

You know, the important stuff.

Like any good parents, we both wanted our definition of what was best for Miles.

I'm sure my husband was frustrated that I wanted to raise a cloth diapering, baby vegan without much consultation for his personal preferences. Perhaps he never envisioned eating buffalo cauliflower with his son while watching the big game. I certainly didn't consider what memories he desired to create with Miles.

Frustrated, we both headed to church with our own visions and dreams for Miles. Upon arrival, a guest preacher mounted the podium. He noticed my belly and smiled. He delivered a dynamic message and in closing asked my husband and I to stand.

He told us, "Children are born a blank canvas.

When they arrive, they have no colors, no paint, nothing that has been imprinted upon them.

Be careful how you paint on your children."

Did you know that there are three different paintings underneath the Mona Lisa? Before finishing one of the most famous paintings in the world, Da Vinci created three others that did not meet his standards.

We don't know why he painted over the three previous paintings nor does the world really care. The majority of us are happy that he did because we have the Mona Lisa as a result, arguably, the most famous painting in the world.

If you look at what has been painted on your life, are you satisfied with the outcome? Are you proud of what you've painted in the lives of others?

If you're not completely at ease with your answer to either of those questions, I encourage you to continue to work on your masterpiece.

Like Da Vinci, who chose to paint over his previous work until he was satisfied with the final outcome, you can do the same.

As you prepare to pick up the paintbrush of your life, you now have the unique opportunity to create your own masterpiece. Our present troubles are the manifestations of seeds sown in our spirits from our past interactions. From a spiritual standpoint, fear, shame, and procrastination are all manifestations of demonic seeds that people have planted in us somewhere on our life's journey. If you don't receive deliverance from those seeds planted, you will be tormented by those demons for the rest of your life.

Every brush stroke is taking control back over your life, your business, your destiny, and sowing a new seed on good ground. Paint over the harsh words people spoke over you, paint over the dream killers, the self defeating thoughts, and anything that is not 100% lined up with the word of God. With scriptures, you can paint over everything covering up God's true vision for your life.

In practice, I want to share an example with you of how I uprooted and painted over the harsh words the enemy spoke over my life.

In 2009, I started going to therapy. After struggling in school and almost flunking out, I was convinced that I was dumb. My therapist assigned a letter writing exercise where I was instructed to write a letter to myself sharing my feelings and emotions. Within the letter I shared my grief and confidence, or lack thereof, in my abilities.

I vividly remember drafting the following sentence: "Confidence in my intellect has seemed to dwindle to obscurity." After reading this one line midway through the letter, my therapist stopped me and said, "Ticora, can you stop? Can you read that again?" I replied, "Sure." She said, "Just that line." I responded, "Confidence in my intellect has seemed to dwindle to obscurity?"

She asked, "How can you think you're stupid and you wrote something like that?"

I was speechless.

In that moment, I could hear a spiritual chain break and crash to the ground. The truth will truly set you free. You may believe lies that your inner voice whisper to you all throughout the day and all throughout the night. You've gotten this far in the book and are possibly hearing whispers of "it worked for her, but it won't work for me" or "you're too damaged to paint over your life canvas."

Do not step into agreement with these thoughts!

Without realizing it, I had stepped into covenant with terrible thoughts about myself that cursed me. Instead of believing that "He makes all things new" according to Revelation 21:5 ESV, I believed that His word didn't apply to me. I could not hear God clearly, because I did not recognize His voice.

His voice was drowned out by my own. On my journey of healing, I had to learn what God sounds like. You cannot hear or discern the Holy Spirit if you cannot recognize His voice. When you step into agreement with the truth, a lie loses all of its power.

As such, I spent time consuming His word and reading scriptures. This allowed me to discern Satan's lies from God's truth.

One exercise that will help you paint a new masterpiece is to write out your lies. Visit ticoradavis.com/resources to access a worksheet to assist you with this exercise.

In one column of the worksheet write out all the lies that you tell yourself, or have accepted from others.

In the opposite column and in response to those lies, write out the truth and the support you have to battle the lie.

For example, if you believe you won't be able to solve a client's unique problem, write in the opposite column instances that you've solved the same or similar problem before. Then, write out all of the support you have on your side to solve the problem. This could be prayer, colleagues, websites, books, your previous results, templates, or even your competition.

This exercise will show you how much God has tipped the scales in your favor. You must battle lies, anxiety, and fear with the truth, your past results, and earthly and spiritual resources.

My dear friend Felicia Kelly always tells me ,"Ticora, go back to the facts." The column to the right and your resources are the facts, and are not the harvest of bad seeds sown in your life.

Your inner voice has you believing these lies when in reality, you're more powerful and positioned to produce now that you are aware.

Sowing seeds is the process of casting seeds over prepared ground.

This book has tilled your soil and planted seeds to shift you into your next level, and activate your creative soul.

You are ready right now to go after your dreams and your next level. As you grow to produce a bountiful harvest, the fruit you bear will nurture the lives of so many people, businesses, corporations and communities.

As others sow into you, you in turn must sow into others.

This book is my seed in your ground.

Reflections from My Past

Prior to publishing this book, I found some of my old writings from January 2016 (approximately four years ago prior to this publication). I was pregnant with my first child, a licensed attorney, searching for my life's purpose, and dealing with depression … again.

As you read the following selection of writings you may see glimpses of yourself in them or maybe it will all seem foreign to you. Either way, I want you to read it and be encouraged by what can happen in a short time (4 years) if you yield to God and implement practical tips to help you in your seasons of being planted.

Excerpts from my journal

Confidence in my potential seems to dwindle to obscurity at times.

In the grand scheme of things, life really isn't that bad. I'm well educated, married to a wonderful man, and my first child is on the way. I have dreams of his face, his laugh, his smile, and wax poetic about how precocious he shall be. How handsome. How the rolls on his legs will remind me of a busted can of biscuits. How he will smell of love and coconut oil and shea butter. How the curls on his head will dance to the sun. How he will be a cooing ball of perfection, much unlike his mother. Much more like how the world views me. Despite the facade of perfection, I feel empty at times.

I have thoughts...they collapse onto me like rubble from an imploded building, tumbling down on me all at once. Bricks hit my back as I run away from the steel beams, plaster, and wood, but smoke-ash, timber and sawdust coat my face. I can't see. Eyes itch with the pain of yesteryear but I run, only to run, back into myself again. Back into my buildings. Back into my towers. Back into my fortress of perfection.

Until it blows up again.

Cause it's only a matter of time before it blows up again.

I just realized something. I'm that girl. Being kind of lost sucks because you're looking for yourself and your purpose on everyone's Instagram page and Pinterest Board. Hours are spent perusing enumerated lists for tips for success, the nighttime and morning routines successful people have, and Steve Harvey quotes. When did he start having the best quotes anyway? I digress. I dive into this treasure hunt daily and nightly hoping to find a beacon of hope at the end of my dark tunnel. If I could just take a pinch of what she did and a dash of what he does and a dollop of grandma's wisdom that will be my own personal recipe for success. Right! Right? Unfortunately, despite being well read and garnering a wealth of useless information I still feel stuck. Like I'm so stuck I need someone to wrap a chain around me to add traction to get me out of this snow covered ditch. Although I'll be free and elated someone reached me, I'll still be bound. And ain't that ironic? To be in bondage to the rescuer who put you in chains? What a sick twist of fate.

I've been writing and have come to the conclusion that I may be depressed. I hate the D word. Depression hovers over you like a drone. It takes aerial shots of you as you walk through life and can take you out at any minute. It clings to your coat tails like a baby duck that's imprinted on you and mistakes you for its mama. It's a parasite you have to constantly watch, otherwise it'll get out of control and wreak havoc on your entire body.

Whew...after reading these excerpts I felt a heaviness in my spirit and a disconnect with the writer...even though the writer was me. I was carrying all of that on me and in me in my planted season. I could not fathom or conceive of what my today would be.

Nor did I realize I was operating in my gift THEN. I wrote so vividly and powerfully in my pain but discounted and overlooked my obvious talent of putting words together. It's so easy to do that in our planted season.

I'll be honest with you, my gift for writing is still being developed. I almost didn't want to release this book, because it wasn't "perfect," but I had to push past those old habits in order to share my message with you.

I want you to know that perfection isn't required for this journey. Action is required. Doing your best is required. Gracing yourself is required as you travel from valleys to your mountain tops.

Following are some practical tools to help you as you move from one shift to the next.

Affirmations

Creativity
I am a co-creator with God. Although every idea I have is divine, I will wisely choose the ideas I will pursue based on my capacity, my tenacity, and potential profitability.

Focus
I am genetically engineered to focus and designed for productivity. If I get off task, I will quickly reroute my hands to do the work I need to do. No task, project, or assignment is too big for me to complete. I will complete every task with ease.

Delegation
God is sending me every person, tool, training, and system I need to work efficiently and effectively in my business. As they come, I will tap into my inner-Moses and appoint godly men and women to manage key tasks and projects. My business is a blessing, but I recognize and accept my responsibility to steward my business so that it does not become a burden.

Attraction
I activate the law of magnetism to attract the people assigned to me and repel anyone and anything not assigned to my life. As what I need comes into my life, I will find ways to use my tools and resources to make more money in less time so that I can enjoy my friends, my family, and my freedom.

The Truth About Time
I have all the time I need to accomplish my daily tasks. Time was created to work for me, not against me. I am in control of my day and will refocus if I get off task. My daily tasks will be accomplished easily and effortlessly.

Boundaries
I am so happy and grateful that I steward my divine gifts and erect healthy boundaries. I am thankful others see God's grace in my life; however, I will not allow anyone or anything to drain my talents to the point where I'm ineffective.

Imposer Syndrome
It's impossible to be an imposter when you are in the will of God. Every room I walk in, I belong in. I always recognize my value even if others fail to do so.

Sample Morning Routine

5:00a - Wake up. Go to bathroom. Drink 1 bottle of water. 10 Minutes of Inspiration (Read 10 pages of a book, listen to 10 minutes of a sermon, or 10 minutes of good music), Read 1 Chapter of The bible, 10x10x10 (10 push ups, 10 sit ups, 10 squats)
5:30a – Shower, Get Dressed, Make up
6:15a – Eat a light breakfast (4oz egg white, 3 oz green peppers and pico de Gallo, 2 tbsp flax seed meal or acai berry bowl)
6:30a – Wake up son, encourage him to eat breakfast and get dressed
7:00a – Pray over my children, my husband and my home
7:30a – Pack the car in preparation of our morning commute
8:00a –In car for commute to sons school
8:30a –Arrival/drop off
8:45a –Head to office or return home for workday
9:00a – Arrive to office, get settled in and prepare morning coffee
9:30a - Morning team huddle, respond to emails, set intention and goals for the day

Your Morning Routine

Use the space provided to write in your sample morning routine

_____

_____

_____

_____

_____

_____

_____

_____

_____

_____

_____

Tips on Productivity, Leadership and Life

Use a time cub when working on tasks. I love the The Miracle TimeCube Timer with 5/15/30/60 which you can easily find on Amazon. My team and I use this TimeCube throughout the workday.

Journal your thoughts for 10 minutes every day, ideally in the evening. Getting your thoughts out in the evening will help you rest more peacefully. When journaling, choose to plan tomorrow today. Review your schedule and list out any weekly tasks you will accomplish. During this nightly time, plan to respond to small tasks during a portion of your day.

Use a calendar (whether digital or physical) to keep your personal and professional days organized.

Develop a consistent morning and evening routine. Although your days will change, your routines should not.

Set out your clothes for tomorrow the night before, including your workout clothing.

Work in 20 minute time blocks with 5-10 minute breaks in between. Use the TimeCube or your phone to track your time. Build up to working in 30 minute time blocks as your endurance builds. Grace yourself for this as it takes time to develop this habit.

Do daily affirmations (goal 10 per day)